DR. PIERRE F. WALTER

THE INNER JOURNEY

How Potential Helps You Find Your True Self

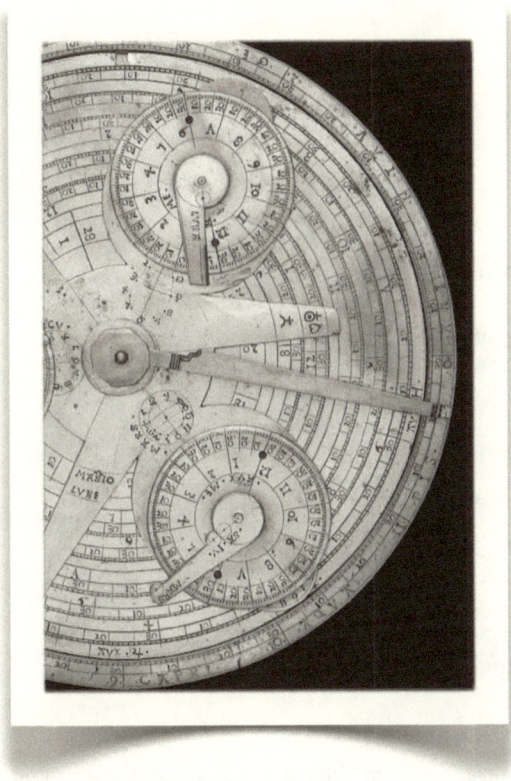

"Articles Series"

Published by Sirius-C Media Galaxy LLC

http://sirius-c-publishing.com

http://siriuscmedia.com

http://ipublica.com

ISBN 978-1-468131-03-1

Contact Information Dr. Pierre F. Walter

publisher@sirius-c-publishing.com

About Dr. Pierre F. Walter

http://drpfw.info

Quotation Suggestion

Pierre F. Walter, *The Inner Journey: How Potential Astrology Helps You Find Your True Self*, Sirius-C Media Galaxy LLC, 2011

About the Author

Pierre F. Walter is an author, international lawyer, researcher, corporate trainer, and lecturer. After finalizing studies in German Law, International Law and *European integration* with diplomas obtained in 1981 through 1983, he graduated in December 1987 at the Law Faculty of the University of Geneva as *Docteur en Droit* in international law.

The doctorate was funded by scholarships from the *Swiss Institute of Comparative Law*, Lausanne, and from the *University of Geneva*, as well as a Fulbright Travel Grant for an assistantship with Professor Louis B. Sohn at *UGA Law School Department of International Law*, Athens, Georgia, USA, in 1985. Pierre F. Walter also served as a research assistant to *Freshfields, Bruckhaus, Deringer,* Cologne, Germany in 1983 and to *Lalive Lawyers,* Geneva, in 1987.

Pierre F. Walter writes and lectures in English, German and French languages; he has written *more than ten thousand pages* embracing all literary genres, including *novels, short stories, film scripts, essays, selfhelp books, monographs* and extended *book reviews*. Also a pianist and composer, he has realized 40 CDs with *jazz, newage* and *relaxation music.*

Pierre F. Walter's professional publications span the domains *International Law, Criminal Law, Holistic Science, Psychology, Education, Shamanism, Ecology, Spirituality, Quantum Physics, Systems Theory, Natural Healing, Peace Research, Personal Growth, Selfhelp* and *Consciousness Research.* 110 Book Reviews, thirty-eight audio books and more than hundred video lectures were realized in the years 2005-2010. Besides, Pierre F. Walter is author and editor of *Great Minds Series*, which features scientists, artists and authors of genius from Leonardo to Fritjof Capra.

Pierre F. Walter publishes via his Delaware firm *Sirius-C Media Galaxy LLC* and the imprints IPUBLICA and Sirius-C Media (SCM).

For Nelson

CONTENTS

Lord we may know what we are,
but know not what we may be.
– William Shakespeare

INTRODUCTION

How did I Come to Do Astrology?

Astrology didn't come to me of late. It didn't come to me as a pastime, or because I was contacted by one of millions of scam artists on the Internet who profess to be serious astrologers but who are just business executives, considering  astrology to be a fashionable new age business. Astrology is a *perennial science* that was developed in the oldest civilizations of humanity and that prospered especially in Babylon, Persia and old Egypt, and later in the Renaissance.

In the 20th century astrology was eventually recognized as a true science and not just a particular mythology and it is today taught at leading universities around the world.

Astrology is a method of exploring ourselves, our relationships and our place within the world. It is thus a primary work tool for gaining self-knowledge. Astrology can give us insight into personal and political situations, from the most intimate to the most mundane. Astrology does not interfere in human destiny and it does by no means follow the wrong doctrine of predestination; it only shows probabilities, potential, the flow of the bioenergy in relationships, tendencies and automatisms, much of it for most people remaining unconscious. A special branch of non-forecasting astrology is so-called karmic or *potential astrology*, which is the branch that I myself practice since more than twenty years.[1]

I am fascinated about Liz Greene's astrological approach since now about twenty years. It all started in Switzerland when I got in touch with a group of astrologers that inscribed in the legacy of 'psychological astrology' founded by Dane Rudyar in the United States and by Alexander Ruperti in Switzerland.

I was doing some social work for them, as they wanted to setup an astrological database in all mental health and law enforcement institutions in the country. With the help of some programmer friends, I was designing for them a software intended for use in all those institutions, and that was easy to handle. The software contained the astrological information from selected books that met the required quality standard, and that were quoted in meticulous detail. The quotes, then, were arranged in the order required for interpreting a birth chart. The software did not contain any module that designed the chart, it was for interpretation purposes only. It was thus left to the individual person to get his or her chart drawn either by a computer program or an astrologer.

---

[1] See, for example, Stephen Arroyo, *Astrology, Karma & Transformation (1992)*, Donna Cunningham, *Healing Pluto Problems (1986)*, Liz Greene, *Saturn (1976), The Astrological Neptune and the Quest for Redemption (1996), The Astrology of Fate (1984),* Liz Greene & Howard Sasportas, *The Luminaries (1992)*, Derek & Julia Parker, *Parker's Astrology (1991)*, Dane Rudyar, *Astrology of Personality (1990), An Astrological Triptych (1991), Astrological Mandala (1994),* Jan Spiller, *Astrology for the Soul (1997).*

Our software was only facilitating the *interpretation* of the chart. The idea was namely that chart interpretation should not be left to computer programs, as the human mind doesn't only proceed logically, as a computer does, but also produces information that is contextual and intuitive. And here, every computer must fail. The final synthesis of a the many vectors contained in birth chart requires *intuition*, and cannot be done by using logical reasoning only.

Both Rudyar and Ruperti were very unusual astrologers. Rudyar was a musician first of all, and Ruperti an osteopathic healer who used astrology as a diagnostic tool for better understanding the underlying psychic causes of his patients' ailments.

Alexander Ruperti

To achieve a true personal maturity is a difficult task at any time, and today it is even more difficult because the whole society is geared to the maintenance of all people in a state of perpetual immaturity, conditioned to buy what the economy has produced. Everything in the modern way of life caters to one's pride and stimulates his sense of greed and envy. It reinforces inherent laziness and complacency, and fosters a basic fear of insecurity. It supports a childish desire to depend on other people or to have one's own way at any cost. Social and moral principles of behavior have lost their authority, and therefore personal contact has become more and more irresponsible. (...) Opportunities for growth which are not fully met leave a residue of unfinished business which must inevitably be dealt with later. That is the real meaning of karma - unfinished business from the past. However, if one does manage to completely fulfill all that life demands of him, there need not be any residue of unfinished business. Achieving this leads to spiritual mastery. Spiritual growth does not stop there, however. If one comes to

the point where he has fulfilled everything he was
meant to do as an individual, then comes the moment
when he will be asked to take on larger responsibilities,
to take on the karma of groups, and eventually of
humanity as a whole.

Both men shared a vision of 'psychological' astrology
that at the time was revolutionary. They said that astrology is
more than just fortune telling, in that it is actually an early
anticipation of what today we call psychology or psychoanalysis, or that we regard as counseling, and that in that
quality, it is to be qualified as *humanistic*. While Rudyar em-
phasized more the humanistic aspect of astrology, Ruperti
spoke more often about psychological astrology. The differ-
ence is merely one of terms.

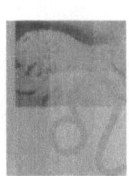 Liz Greene inscribes in this tradition while she
goes one step ahead. She calls her astrological
approach 'mythological' because, farther than
Rudyar and Ruperti, she has integrated her psy-
choanalytical and mythological knowledge in
astrology, which is basically knowledge of all the
myths that have moved and modulated humanity since the
starting point of human conscious evolution, around fifty
thousand years ago.

POTENTIAL ASTROLOGY

The Star Script

Introduction

In the previous chapter, I have shortly mentioned astrology as a life guide tool. Here, I would like to give you some more details on *potential astrology*. To begin with, I have developed my own approach to potential astrology inspired by the Swiss school of psychological astrology[2] which was initiated by Dane Rudyar's *humanistic astrology*, and evolved around highly qualified astrologers such as Alexander Ruperti[3], Stephen Arroyo[4] and Liz Greene.[5]

As I already mentioned above, potential astrology does no forecasting, but uses the astrological method and vocabulary as tools for helping clients to find their life's mission and their innate talents and capacities by a karmic analysis of the birth chart, mainly by examining the *moon nodes* as well as the *prenatal and postnatal eclipses*. If we do away with prejudice and look at human history, we see that both coaching and astrology have their basis in long-standing traditions.

---

[2] It is propagated today under the header *Astrodienst* and based in Zurich, Switzerland and does the larger part of its consultations through its well-visited web presence, astrodienst.com.

[3] See, for example, Alexander Ruperti, *Cycles of Becoming (1978)*.

[4] See, for example, Stephen Arroyo, *Astrology, Karma & Transformation (1993)*.

[5] See, for example, Liz Greene, *Astrology of Fate (1986)*.

Modern coaching has its roots originally in the business virtues of the industrial age, but it can be traced back to Antiquity. The rules of success and ethics have never changed, in fact, because they are fundamental rules of life and living. Astrology was in Antiquity considered as the *Queen of all Sciences*, a royal tool for looking up the mysterious interconnections between the human and the divine conditions, so as to

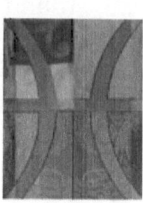 find out about the right way of living at a certain time, within a certain context and at a certain place. I explain this so carefully because there is lots of misinformation today about astrology; in fact, most of what you find today is a modern form of vulgarized astrology that is heavily influenced by commercial interests rather than the desire to provide competent spiritual support for the truth-seeker.

Let me therefore shortly elucidate where humanistic astrology originates from and what its purpose is. Humanistic astrology is part of *perennial astrology*, a millenary spiritual tradition that in antiquity was part of the hermetic *corpus scientia* that the philosopher or sage studied. As such, it was a holy science, a precious tool leading to cosmic knowledge and a good starting point for gaining self-knowledge. Astrology was not dissected from astronomy yet; the two ways of projecting macroscopic events were complementary sources of knowledge.

Karmic astrology draws a diagram of our soul including our former life karma. It clearly indicates the marking trails and traits of our unconscious and our conscious personalities, not only the one that we show like a mask to the outside world, and which is our *persona*, but also the selves that we bear inside of us and most of which are still virgin or in a state of potentiality. But it's those *inner selves*, to repeat it, that carry most of our creative energy.

Your birth chart shows your unique potential, which your talents are and how you can possibly realize them, provided you are willing to invest the energy to achieve this goal.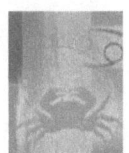

Working since years with voice dialogue, I know how important it is to develop awareness about our *inner shadow*, the hidden or repressed parts of our self, the energies that are lost to our consciousness because they are not admitted, like haunting shades of smoke in front of our inner eye. It is the energies, the desires and the drives we deny and reject, thereby cutting off their link with our conscious self. The truth is that these rejected and denied energies drive us much more than the ones we admit and acknowledge, but since we put them under the magic spell of taboo, we project their shadows onto others. This leads to the result that we see the bad man always in others or in peoples, in groups or even, very generally, the 'bad world' as opposed to 'good heaven'. This process is known as the triple effect of *repression-regression-projection*, resulting in blinding out what we deny in ourselves, and in projecting it upon others, or a group of scapegoats.

An essential step in your search for truth is to acknowledge, to admit and to *face your shadow*. Astrology offers you a map to explore your inner landscape. This map is genuine and accurate, and it reflects all your inner energies.

 Many of us today are open to see the truth about themselves, some of them desperately longing for a source of wisdom that is independent of gurus and sects. Astrology is here the number one resource to begin with. Potential astrology is one possible map to approach your inner landscape because it reveals to you your unique soul power. It is for this reason that I have termed the individual karmic or potential astrology chart our *Star Script*.

The Star Script

But then if I do not strive, who will?

– CHUANG TZU

Today we are at the end of centuries of fragmentation and analysis and there is a general striving for *synthesis* in all walks of life, in all sciences, in all arts. Much as in the *Renaissance*. This is the reason why today so many methods and approaches come up. In fact, most of them are not new, but replicas of old concepts that we have forgotten.

In Antiquity, astrology was part of the hermetic *corpus scientia* that the philosopher or sage studied. As such, it was a sacred science, a part of cosmic knowledge and a tool for self-knowledge. To repeat it, astrology was not dissected from astronomy; the two ways of projecting macroscopic events were complementary sources of  knowledge. Astrology was an integral part of perennial philosophy, the queen of all sciences. It was unthinkable, even still in the Middle Ages, that an erudite or sage would not study astrology and excel in it whether for personal or mundane forecasting, or just for learning about cosmic laws.

The past millennium was perhaps the culmination point of ignorance in the whole run of human history. The Church's absolute power quest was based upon the ignorance of the common believer, and therefore knowledge became a form of subversion, generally knowledge about the roots and functions of life, and in particular self-knowledge. However, we can see that astrology went all the way through to us, from ancient times until today, and astrologers were among the wisest people in the world. Johannes Kepler (1571–1630) was known to be an excellent astrologer, Isaac Newton (1643–1727) is said to have had solid knowledge about not only astronomy but also astrology. And Nostradamus, the French astrologer and prophet Michel de Nostredame (1503–1566), was one of the most powerful psychics and visionaries of all times. He was the personal consultant of kings and queens and the basis of all his psychic power was astrology.[6]

In the 19th and 20th centuries, astrology became more and more vulgarized and the use of the true astrology remained a knowledge tool for a minority of educated and spiritual individuals while the majority became more and more indoctrinated by the mass media to believe in a reductionist form of it – rainbow press astrology. Today, there is a profound split between true astrology which is a science, and

---

[6] See Pierre F. Walter, *Divination Basics, Scholarly Article (2011).*

popular astrology which is gossip and fake or at best a pleas-

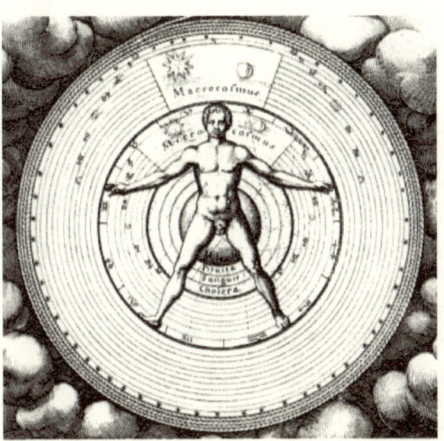

ant social game.

This is why not only myself, but many serious astrologers are have to *distance ourselves* from people who make money on the ignorance and the greediness of the masses. This differ-ence is both on the competence level and on the motivation level. Astrology is a science and an art that requires not only intelligence and commitment, but also strong intuitive and associative thinking capacities, as well as a profound basic knowledge of mythology, psychology and psychoanalysis. It is concerned with truth and helping people to identify and accept the truth of their greater life cycle and cosmic identity.

What you get in popular press and on the Internet, for the most part, is neither truth nor is there any commitment from the side of those who do it. It is fake from the first to the last in that only one or two chart vectors of more than one hundred are considered and taken for the absolute truth, without caring for the individual astrological chart of the person. Telling you that you are a *Gemini* by your sun sign does not reveal you anything about yourself since there are millions of people in every country that are born in the sign of Gemini.

Serious astrologers are not motivated by money gain or to appear in fashionable media, but solely by the positive impact that their work may have on prospective clients, an impact that ideally helps them to live with a greater sense of identity, to derive more satisfaction from the effective realization of their unique talents, to live a life that is more balanced and more healthy and to use their resources in a way that their high-energy input comes back to them in a transformed form, as money, fame and recognition. This, and only this is the true reward of the astrological work and profession.

Until these days, most people think that astrology was either some kind of leisure game or else a form of charlatanism. However, with the turn of the millennium, a raising minority of people become interested in the true and originally scientific use of astrology in its purest form. In fact, the *Aquarius Age* will be again oriented toward self-knowledge and individualized forms of spirituality and astrology will then play a leading role in the quest of the individual to reconnect with the self and its higher cosmic octave.

Here I shall explain what I mean when I talk about *Potential Astrology*. I use this term as my own creation and define it below. It is a branch of astrology that is not divinatory but revelatory in character,  in that it deals with the revelation of the client's unique life mission, and that mirrors to the client their special karmic gifts and talents ideally to be realized in this life cycle. Ancient Greek philosophers, and among them especially *Socrates*, spoke in this context about the *daimon* of an individual which could also be called the cosmic imprint of the soul. Knowing this cosmic fingerprint in our cosmic life cycle and development through karmic astrology is a unique opportunity for personal growth.

We do not incarnate as blank books. Potential Astrology is a particular branch of astrology that deals exclusively with the birth chart looking for the unique gifts and talents of the person, by preference a newborn, an infant, a toddler or school child or an adolescent, their power potential and the areas where they can possibly realize it to its fullest. This kind of astrology starts from the insight that there is karma, which simply is cause-and-effect, and that as a result of that, we all come with an agenda, when we incarnate in this world.

This agenda is a mix between elements we can't control and that are karmic, and elements that we have put, by choice, before we decided to incarnate. Potential Astrology is thus can be said to be *a diagnostic tool* for the life consultant in order for them to know the particular inner maps of the client. The life consultant does not do any forecasting and this is what distinguishes him or her from the astrologer.

This is at least how I myself define my role. Our central goal in potential astrology is to assist people in their quest for leading happy and fulfilled lives in maximizing the effectiveness with which they realize and deploy their specific talents and character strengths while, at the same time, minimizing character weaknesses and misbalances.

I put it in the formula that *every child is Buddha*. Potential Astrology serves as a mirror to reflect our hidden potential. It is therefore a precious tool for those who desire to know more about themselves, or of the destiny and the unique possibilities of their children or children in their care.

The birth chart reveals where our talents are and how we can possibly realize them, provided we are willing to invest the energy needed to achieve this goal. In fact, potential astrology draws a soul pictogram

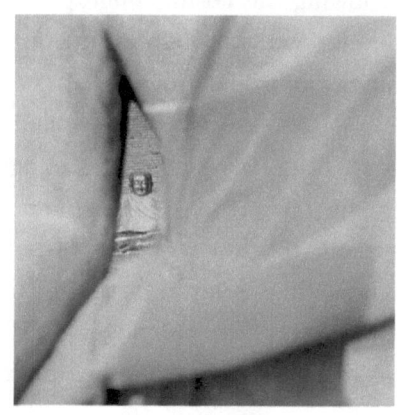

that includes the karma and dharma of the soul. It clearly indicates the traits of our unconscious and our conscious personalities, not only the ones that we show like a mask to the outside world (*persona*, old Greek, means mask), but also the personalities that we bear inside of us (and try to hide) and that represent our shadow and most of which are still virgin or in a state of potential. This entity in us has been called by the old Greek the *daimon*, and it has been given a name in all the ancient wisdom traditions.

Let me now explain a little more in detail the most common vectors examined in a potential astrology chart:

▸ Character and Talents

▶   Life Lessons

▶   Karma Lessons

Character and Talents

The first broad area that potential astrology looks at is the *character and the talents* of the client. Every soul comes with a *special and unique potential of talents and skills* when it incarnates for a particular lifetime. These talents have been developed and worked on either during one or several life cycles. Some talents are in a state of virginity or potentiality when the soul incarnates, which means that their realization is intended by the soul, and by the specific constellation of energies, their realization is indeed highly probable. Yet they are not yet real in the sense that they need to be worked on by constant practice, refinement and mature realization.

Character is a special mixture of male/female energies and energies from the four elements (fire, water, wind, earth), as well as *planetary energies* that have molded a certain thought, emotion and behavior pattern. This pattern is distinct in the birth chart and it can be seen in which ways it has developed from former life cycles and in which way it is supposed to evolve according to the cosmic life plan.

This part of the analysis also deals with particular obstructions, energy blockages and misbalances that lead or have led to karmic challenges and/or life lessons. Karmic astrology can reveal what exactly those particular blockages are and in which areas of your life they are located. Generally, if you refuse to work on those issues, stagnation and/or health problems, accidents and other 'misfortunes' tend to happen until consciousness is mature enough to face the issues.

Life Lessons

Life Lessons are created by the soul in order to become more perfect and pure. You can imagine them as something like a plan that we have made up before we incarnated. Let me formulate one of my own life lessons:

    – In this life cycle I wish to become more autonomous. I wish to dissolve attachments and bonds that keep me enslaved in unhealthy relationships that chain my development and evolution. At the same time I wish to learn what healthy and constructive relationships are like and how to build such relationships. This is valid for both the private and professional sphere.

The problem is that we generally forget about our life plan after we incarnate. Only highly evolved souls such as, for example, Tibetan Lamas can remember them. This makes us believe that life lessons are 'fallen from heaven' in order to 'punish' us. Nothing is farther from reality! We have full control about how to accomplish our life lessons once we have rendered them conscious and accept them.

Potential astrology helps us identify, recognize, acknowledge and fully accept our life lessons so as to face and master them. The key of tremendous success in many lives can be seen in facing particular life lessons and 'thus turning the bad into good', a process that is most often accompanied by more or less strong anxiety.

Karmic Challenges

Karmic Challenges are life lessons from former lives that have not been met and thus been taken over into the present life cycle.

Thus, these are past issues that however have an impact on the present life cycle, either through unconscious or half-conscious remembrance, repeated dreams, patterns in behavior or relationships that are self-repeating (and often self-defeating) or a general lack of success or power in life.

You may resent karma lessons as something like a magic spell that has been cast upon your life and that is more or less difficult to identify let alone remove without astrological, therapeutic or otherwise spiritual help. However, karma lessons are neither magical nor mysterious but are the mere result from our own past choices that, in most cases, we have forgotten or overridden by subsequent options or interests. They can be residues of forgotten projects that are unfulfilled yet necessary in order to complete soul lessons, or they can result from hurts or injustice inflicted to others and/or self.

Potential astrology helps to consciously recognize and face karmic challenges so that they are easier to be dealt with and met constructively and creatively. This is by far a better way than just passively suffering them.

Hereafter, I shall explain the meaning of *Inner Maps*. Our inner landscape is a particularly important vector in potential astrology. It is a synonym for what I use to call our *soul pictogram*. This is a metaphor for the fact that every birth chart contains a *unique set of parameters* that are related to each other and that form something like a hologram or *holographic picture* about the individual. It's what you may call the cosmic imprint of the soul. It's like an energy code that is unique and that identifies that individual soul.

Inner Maps

Astrology is but one possible tool to explore our inner landscape or inner maps. And it is an accurate one. Other maps are psychoanalysis or transactional analysis or the inner dialogue, or, to cite more esoteric ones, the *Tarot* or the *I Ching*, or else the *Runes* or *Geomancy*.[7] All divinations are pro-

---

[7] Id.

jection systems to mirror the *content of consciousness* in a way that is intelligible for our rational mind. There is nothing supernatural about this quest, and all the fuss about those forms of knowledge being silly or charlatanism are the pure results of ignorance. It is a fact that potential astrology renders a comprehensive map of our inner landscape.

Since quite a few years people from the West travel the globe in order to acquire self-knowledge; they go far in order to see what is very close. The truth is

that they search for a map. They know the landscape is there but they think they could not explore it without a map reader, *a guru*. This opinion is not wrong, obviously. One who has gone the way can show you the way. But this way he shows to you will be his way – *not your way*. There are two others possibilities.

First, you can gain wisdom without a map, and second, you can become your own map reader. Doing without a map may be possible after years of serious energy work, as for example Zen meditation, yoga, Qigong or Tai Chi; however the influence of our quite nature-hostile culture is not to underestimate.[8] Often sages who reach that level of consciousness have lived through a childhood full of magic and

---

[8] See Pierre F. Walter, *Alternative Medicine and Wellness Techniques, Scholarly Article (2011)*.

poverty which made that their basic nutrition was vegetarian. They may have suffered from early abuse as the example Krishnamurti clearly shows, but were strong enough to survive all those hardships with a strong and innocent heart.

The other way, which I recommend to you, is that you become your own map reader. Please consider what two renowned and respected sages say, J. Krishnamurti and Ramana Maharshi, and that I can summarize as follows:

- You are able to explore your inner landscape without a guru;

- You do not need to reject a map as long as you keep your vision;

- You can reach your destination just by keeping your focus;

- You need to develop passive awareness of your thoughts, dreams and actions.

These sages thus affirm that we are able to go the way on our own, that we can take supporting maps as long as we keep our vision intact and do not take the finger for the moon, or the map for the landscape. They stress the need for us to develop attentiveness, passive awareness of our inner and outer processes and the whole process of life. There is only one truth but different ways to reach it. And there is only one truth that is *yours*. Yet there are different ways to reach it. There may be a way that is more effective than the others, because it is more direct and does not waste time and resources.

Potential astrology may be this way for you. Once you see that, you are less dogmatic in your choice of maps. You know that you have enough autonomy to not confuse the land-scape and the map, and take the support that serves you best for the journey to your own self. And when you un-derstand that as a good thing for yourself, why  not wanting to offer it to your child, a child of a befriended family, or a child in your care as an educator?

Before you learn the knowledge that will reveal to you your unique life lessons and karma lessons, and the basic framework of your life's mission, I invite you to use your own inner wisdom, your intuition, to find some clues about the destination of your greater life cycle. You may have got hints already, perhaps in your childhood, perhaps later, that were pointing to your unique tasks and mission.

The Intuitive Way

The *intuitive way to gain self-knowledge* works in my experience best with establishing a feedback loop with your inner selves. I invite you thus to go on an inner journey, which is a self-exploratory quest, and to use your intuition for finding out about your own truth, your own uniqueness, and your own gifts and talents.

What is intuition? Here is a little quiz about what you think is intuition. You may skip this section if intuition has already a firm place in your life and go directly to the following one. But if you have doubts about intuition being able to reveal you real secrets about your life and your destiny, then please do the quiz. In the answers you will find some important clues about what intuition represents and what it can do for you.  I have consciously *not put radio buttons* as they give an either-or choice. In life there is seldom an either-or, but much more of a fusion between things. So, sometimes you may well choose both answers expressing that you agree half and disagree half, or that you see the point half-way, but remain half-way undecided or skeptical.

Affirmation One

When I inquire into what intuition possibly is or means, I find first of all that it is useful as a quality.

True   Not True

Affirmation Two

When I think that I can know a lot of things from books, a voice inside tells me that somehow I knew all this already, even as early as in childhood.

True   Not True

Affirmation Three

In school I never heard anything about intuition. This seems to be a subject that is blinded out officially in our culture. On the other hand, I know some successful people who follow their inner voice in all important decisions.

True   Not True

Affirmation Four

I know that if there is something like intuition, I surely was gifted with that as a child but somehow from the moment I joined school I began to lose it or forget about it.

True   Not True

Affirmation Five

Intuition is something I'd like to learn if it can be learnt, or discover within myself. I have observed that artists follow a special way when they create their art, perhaps it's that?

True   Not True

Affirmation Six

I think we all use intuition once in a while in those moments when we don't know for sure what to do, or not to do.

True   Not True

Affirmation Seven

In the old sagas it is often said that the hero threw the dice to ask for the way to go. King David, in the Bible, is reported to have done it, and quite often. This is probably a way to get our subconscious mind involved in the decision-making process, and this in turn is only another expression for using intuition.

True   Not True

Affirmation Eight

Women are said to have more intuition than men. If this is true or not is very difficult to verify. But when using this affirmation as a metaphor, it's true. We all have male and female energies in us, or *yang* and *yin*. Intuition clearly is a quality related to our right brain hemisphere, as it has to do with *associative thinking*, that is the way the right brain works, contrary to the linear logical thinking of the left brain hemisphere. And the right brain, in turn, is a primary *yin* area of the body while the left brain hemisphere is a primary *yang* area.[9]

True   Not True

---

[9] Id.

Affirmation Nine

As far as I can think back in my life, I have never used intuition. I have always been logical, and I always used logical straightforward linear thinking to get results, and for the rest have consulted books or affirmed authorities to get the knowledge I need. All the rest is humbug and charlatanism.

True   Not True

Your Life's Mission

Here you are going to respond in a particular way writing down your answers in stream-of-consciousness writing style, *as fast as you can*, and without caring about orthography, spelling and casing. This means you kind of overrun your intellectual mind and let your gut or unconscious answer for you. Needless to say that you should not think anything when doing this. When you finish reading the questions, ideally without even one second having elapsed, you are spitting out your answer!

My Life's Mission

Here you are revealing to yourself what you know deep inside of you, in a place that you may not be able to identify so far. This place is your gut or intuitive mind. It is also called unconscious or subconscious mind in the language of psychoanalysis. This place in you *knows all the answers to all questions* you may possibly come up with. It possesses a unique knowledge that is inborn in that it does not need to be learnt.

> At various occasions in my life, as early as in childhood, I got hints, thoughts, feelings and insights about a wonderful direction my life was going to take. It was

like that special thing or profession I wanted to do had a particular taste. There was so much space in it, so much latitude and beauty. In addition, there were synchronistic events happening at times that seemed to direct my attention toward that matter, field of interest, activity or particular knowledge. It showed me that I was particularly gifted or interested to engage in. Jot down your thoughts in a few seconds...

Your Child's Vision

Here you are going to respond in a particular way writing down your answers in stream-of-consciousness writing style, as fast as you can, and without car-ing about orthogra-

phy, spelling and casing. This means you kind of overrun your intellectual mind and let your gut or subconscious an-swer for you. Needless to say that you should not think any-thing when doing this. When you finish reading the ques-tions, ideally without even one second having elapsed, you are spitting out your answer!

My Child's Vision

I use the expression *Child's Vision* intently in a double sense. I mean by it both the vision you had as a child, and the vision of your inner child. We all had moments in childhood where we suddenly thought we will be going to become a bus driver, pilot, doctor, nurse or famous writer and artist, politi-cian or revolutionary, and later often forgot about these hints. Most often, our parents and educators overlooked them as well with the result that we entered our adulthood as a virgin in all senses of the word, a *tabula rasa*, emptied of all what was true in us, forgotten and destroyed by a nonsensical and ruthless education. What happened for most of us was that this valuable content that we possessed as a child was being replaced by fake, that is book knowledge and idiotic assumptions.

You can find the way back to the vision you had as a child and that now is the vision of your inner child, the entity in you that preserved that special knowledge and that is accessible to you when you relax and focus inside.

This is the vision I had as a child about myself and my future, and the vision my inner child has preserved so that I can intuitively feel it now. Jot down your thoughts in a few seconds…

Your Moon Nodes

One of the most important vectors to be used in karmic and potential astrology are the so-called *Moon Nodes*. The Moon Nodes are very complex astronomical intersection points of both the Moon's and Earth's, and Earth's and Sun's trajectories. Whatever they represent in astronomy and what their natural reason is does not interest the astrologer. Astrology is a metaphor in the sense that it derives

meaning and results from natural events without suffering from the obsession of natural scientists to analyze and understand these events. For most people a rather esoteric matter in astrology, the Moon Nodes are a reliable indicator for karmic challenges and they help reveal, together with other indications in the chart, our unique life mission. They show how vital energies in your chart and your life flow – or not flow!

The Moon Nodes establish an important axis in the birth chart because they are always opposite to each other. This axis highly energizes and enhances the Signs and Houses touched by it thus giving them special importance for your life and your development. The South Node (SN), also called *Dragon Tail, ketu* or *negative karma*, describes our weaknesses and excesses depending on thought and action automatisms established in former life cycles.

The North Node (NN), also called *Dragon Head, rahu* or *positive karma* designates the dharma and new behavior to adopt during the present life cycle that will bring more harmony and true happiness.

The South Node (SN) points to where you are coming from while the North Node (NN) points to where you are going to. You can also say that the South Node (SN) indicates your karma and resulting *Karma Lessons* while the North Node (NN) indicates your *Dharma* and your developmental potential for the present and future evolution. You can also say that your South Node (SN) is what you should strive away from and that your North Node (NN) is what you should strive toward in your present incarnation. So the direction you should take in your present life cycle is to move from the SN to the NN by adopting more and more of the characteristics and qualities of the NN and letting go more and more the characteristics of your SN.

Finally it can be said that the integration of the Moon Nodes in a conscious life is something not static, but dynamic. The advantage of Moon Nodes analysis is that the chance of error is rather low since there is a *consensus* among astrologers from around the world as to the significance of every of the twelve constellations Nodes in Signs and the twelve other constellations Nodes in Houses.

Another advantage of the Moon Nodes is their high focus. I would say if you have no time to see anything else in a chart, or if the client does not want to have a long interpretation, restrict yourself to establishing the Moon Nodes.

In my practice, I begin astrological consultations always with the result of my Moon Nodes analysis. This is recommended because imbalances in the general setup of someone's life can be seen immediately. To use an image from holistic medicine: any imbalance in our lifestyle leaves a trace in our body, so that we can say that every illness is nothing but the result of an imbalance. This is a hint to the importance of balance and harmony in all what we think and do.

Generally, for the interpretation, we can say that the South Node (SN) indicates the past karma or the qualities or characteristics we should reduce while the North Node (NN) indicates the future or the qualities or characteristics we should enhance. Thus, the Nodal Axis clearly represents a direction in the chart.

Karmic astrologers stress that the *cycle of death and rebirth* is so strict that destiny uses the first twenty years of each life in order to reconstitute consciously our former personality of which our memory has stored only automatisms and behavior codes that were once our key forms of conduct. Normally, those elements of our memory are deeply unconscious while they are coded in the DNA. Before we incarnate, we choose with the utmost care our family, parents and educators that have exactly the qualities, the behavior and the knowledge, but also the deficiencies and ignorance that we need to work on our karma so as to realign it with cosmic law and harmony.

- ▸ We choose all in life.

- ▸ There is no destiny just falling upon us.

- ▸ Seen from this perspective, there are no bad news.

- ▸ What we can do is to raise our consciousness level.

- ▸ Then our choices become conscious choices.

- ▸ Potential astrology helps with this quest.

As a result, later on in life, changes occur. Between our twenties and our forties we *basically live in conformity with our old karmic patterns*, either by conforming or by opposing our parents. It is by living through all this again, that we render the unconscious content of our consciousness (the automatisms and non-reflected upon ways of conduct) conscious so that we can see where our errors are and our impasses. This is the way most major crashes in life occur within our forties with the high chance that we redirect our lives positively.

One last word about what many people misunderstand about astrology. As the old adage says *The Stars Incline, But they Do Not Determine*, astrology has nothing to do with what fanatic Calvinism called predestination.[10]

It is more of a mirror. It shows us how we project ourselves onto the cosmic surface and it reflects us the consequences. We are still the actors, and we can even re-enact our whole life by just changing what we think today, *hic et nunc.* And we may live the contrary of what  was to be seen in our birth chart. Krishnamurti has said something similar and it was for this reason that he was not much fond of astrology, but in my view he was too absolutist in this point. Most people, generally, take most things for granted instead of questioning them and asking if this or that information fits in our truth, or not. That is the danger K saw in astrology and, generally, in all divination.[11]

Of course, bad astrologers will not serve the reputation of good astrology nor clients who eat all what they get to

---

[10] See Pierre F. Walter, *Natural Order, Monograph (2010)*, Chapter Two.

[11] See Pierre F. Walter, *Divination Basics, Scholarly Article (2011)*.

hear from others, including astrologers. Everything can be used stupidly or wisely.

▶ Learn to choose consciously

▶ As a result chances will be higher that you hit the right goals

Astrology doesn't interfere in our life; it only shows *probabilities, potential, energetic relationships, tendencies* and *automatisms*, much of what for most people remains unconscious. It is for this reason that astrology represents such a wonderful tool for *starting the journey into a more conscious way of life*, one that is based upon self-knowledge. Applying this wisdom to education, you may want to help your child or a child in your care to make choices, and to make them more consciously. Potential astrology is a valuable tool on the way to raise your child's consciousness level, by enhancing their focus on their true gifts and talents, thereby minimizing the risk to miss one's life mission or to fail in one's later career.

GLOSSARY

Contextual Glossary

Perennial Science

I would like to elucidate some of the elements that both perennial philosophy and postmodern science share, as ingredients of a soup that today we call *holistic science*. My desire is to show that there are basically *twelve*, and probably more, ingredients and characteristics of holistic science that are presently more and more embraced, as we mature into new science which is of course just a newer vintage of very old and perennial science. These twelve emanations or branches of the tree of knowledge remain still forbidden to most humans today because they follow the oversoul of the mass media, instead of following their own lucid inner voice. Ancient traditional cultures and their scientific traditions, and what we today call perennial philosophy were holistic; they embraced flow principles, and they were truly scientific. They looked at life as a *Gestalt*, and derived conclusions from the observation of the living and moving, not from the dead.

Here are the twelve branches of the ancient tree of knowledge[12]:

- Science and Divination

- Science and Energy

- Science and Flow

- Science and Gestalt

- Science and Intent

- Science and Intuition

- Science and Knowledge

- Science and Pattern

- Science and Perception

- Science and Philosophy

- Science and Truth

- Science and Vibration

Inner Selves

Generalities

Inner Selves are energies in our psyche that form part of our total and integral wholeness. In the ideal case, they

---

[12] See, more extensively in *Walter's Encyclopedia, Academic Edition (2010).*

should be balanced and in harmony with each other. This means that all inner selves ideally should work in synch, as a sort of *inner team*. It is essential that all members of this inner team are fully awake and communicate with each other. In most people's psyche, however, the inner child is somnolent or asleep, and either the inner parent or the inner adult are hypertrophied and dominate the psyche.

While the truth about our inner selves goes back to Antiquity, the insight in modern times has been made fruitful for psychiatry through Eric Berne in 1950, the founder of Transactional Analysis (TA). Eric Berne recognized three essential inner selves: *Inner Child, Inner Parent and Inner Adult*. In my own research and work with the inner dialogue during an Erickson hypnotherapy, I encountered the presence of additional entities such as the *Inner Controller* or *Inner Critic* as the instance in the psyche that represents the societal, cultural and moralistic values that we have internalized through education and conditioning. If the Inner Controller hijacks the psyche, we are unable to realize our love desires. In addition to these inner selves, I encountered an entity of superior wisdom that I called *Lux* and a shadow entity I called *Sad King* and which embodied repressed emotions that had turned into sadistic drives.

Inner Child

Inner Child is a psychic entity, part-personality, or psychic energy, created between our 7th and 14th year of life, and that is part of our *inner triangle*. Positively, the inner child energy is primarily emotional and wistful, predominantly creative. It is the motor of every human being's creativity. It can be said to be the creative motor, the very source energy in humans that makes that we can be spontaneous, creative and sometimes a little mad, to go beyond the limiting framework of the rational and repetitive mind. Negatively, the inner child is either mute or cataleptic so that its energy cannot manifest, or else its energy is turned upside-down which makes an inner child that is rebellious, capricious, willful or overbearing, producing the 'clochard' personality, the 'hippie', the 'anarchist', the 'eternal student' and abuser of the social system.

Inner Adult

Inner Adult is a psychic entity, part-personality or psychic energy that represents our logical thinking, our reason, our maturity. Positively, it makes for our balanced decisions, our down-to-earth attitude and our sense for daily responsibilities. Negatively, the inner adult manifests as the intellectual nerd or through emotional frigidity, cynicism or an obsession to measure human relations on a scale of reasonableness or straightness without considering the emotional dimension. The hypertrophied inner adult energy plays a major role in modern education where it results in devastating damage on the next generations' emotional integrity. The hypertrophied inner adult also produces the 'professional skeptic', the obnoxious 'total rationalist' who considers ten percent of the human nature as predominantly important, flushing the other ninety percent down the toilet!

Inner Parent

Inner Parent is a psychic entity, part-personality or psychic energy that represents our inner value standards, our moral attitudes, our caring for self and others, but negatively also our judging others, our I-know-better attitude or blunt interference into the lives of others without regard for their privacy. The hypertrophied inner parent energy plays a dominant role in tyrannical and persecutory societal, religious and political systems. Nowadays, it plays a major role within our abuse-centered culture, in the stringently paranoid child protection industry that managed to turn international adoption down over the last two decades in almost all jurisdictions of the world.

Inner Dialogue

The *inner dialogue* is a technique to get in touch with our inner selves through relaxation or self-hypnosis and subsequent dialogues with one or several of our inner selves, in a state of light trance. The state of light trance can be self-induced, with no facilitator needed, and outside of a psychotherapy. The inner dialogue should ideally be fixed on paper, at least in the beginning, because the voices that come up, are very soft and writing down the dialogues helps to keep focus. The technique is also called *Voice Dialogue*, for example by Stone & Stone, in their book *Embracing Our Selves (1982)*. However, the expression could mislead novice users as the 'voices' are not really voices of course, as they are not to be heard with our ears, but something like intuitions, or flashes of intuition, or sudden precisely formulated thoughts that seem to come 'from nowhere'.

Intuition

Intuition is inner knowledge that typically manifests spontaneously and that is all-wise and non-judgmental, broad in scope and wistful; typically, intuition is transpersonal in intent, not ego-based, thus manifesting something like cosmic intention. [13]

---

[13] See Pierre F. Walter, *The Idiot Guide on Intuition, Awareness Guide (2010)*, Part Two.

BIBLIOGRAPHY

Contextual Bibliography

Arntz, William & Chasse, Betsy

What the Bleep Do We Know
20th Century Fox, 2005 (DVD)

Down The Rabbit Hole Quantum Edition
20th Century Fox, 2006 (3 DVD Set)

Bleep
An der Schnittstelle von Spiritualität und Wissenschaft
Verblüffende Erkenntnisse und Anstösse zum Weiterdenken
Berlin: Vak Verlag, 2007

Arroyo, Stephen

Astrology, Karma & Transformation
The Inner Dimensions of the Birth Chart
Sebastopol, CA: CRSC Publications, 1978

Astrologie, Karma und Transformation
Die Chancen schwieriger Aspekte
Frankfurt/M: Heyne Verlag, 1998

Relationships and Life Cycles
Astrological Patterns of Personal Experience
Sebastopol, CA: CRCS Publications, 1993

Handbuch der Horoskop-Deutung
Berlin: Rowohlt, 1999

Bachelard, Gaston

The Poetics of Reverie
Translated by Daniel Russell
Boston: Beacon Press, 1971

Poetik des Raumes
Frankfurt/M: Fischer Verlag, 2001

Balter, Michael

The Goddess and the Bull
Catalhoyuk, An Archaeological Journey
to the Dawn of Civilization
New York: Free Press, 2006

Bandler, Richard

Get the Life You Want
The Secrets to Quick and Lasting Life Change
With Neuro-Linguistic Programming
Deerfield Beach, Fl: HCI, 2008

Blofeld, J.

The Book of Changes
A New Translation of the Ancient Chinese I Ching
New York: E.P. Dutton, 1965

Blum, Ralph H. & Laughan, Susan

The Healing Runes
Tools for the Recovery of Body, Mind, Heart & Soul
New York: St. Martin's Press, 1995

Bohm, David

Wholeness and the Implicate Order
London: Routledge, 2002

Die implizite Ordnung
Grundlagen eines dynamischen Holismus
München: Goldmann Wilhelm, 1989

Thought as a System
London: Routledge, 1994

Quantum Theory
London: Dover Publications, 1989

La plénitude de l'univers
Paris: Rocher, 1992

Branden, Nathaniel

How to Raise Your Self-Esteem
New York: Bantam, 1987

Die 6 Säulen des Selbstwertgefühls
Erfolgreich und zufrieden durch ein starkes Selbst
München: Piper Verlag, 2009

Butler-Bowden, Tom

50 Success Classics
Winning Wisdom for Work & Life From 50 Landmark Books
London: Nicholas Brealey Publishing, 2004

Boldt, Laurence G.

Zen and the Art of Making a Living
A Practical Guide to Creative Career Design
New York: Penguin Arkana, 1993

How to Find the Work You Love
New York: Penguin Arkana, 1996

Zen Soup
Tasty Morsels of Zen Wisdom From Great Minds East & West
New York: Penguin Arkana, 1997

The Tao of Abundance
Eight Ancient Principles For Abundant Living
New York: Penguin Arkana, 1999

Das Tao der Fülle
Vom Reichtum, der uns glücklich macht
Mittelberg: Joy Verlag, 2001

Cain, Chelsea & Moon Unit Zappa

Wild Child
New York: Seal Press (Feminist Publishing), 1999

Calderone & Ramey

Talking With Your Child About Sex
New York: Random House, 1982

Campbell, Joseph

The Hero With A Thousand Faces
Princeton: Princeton University Press, 1973
(Bollingen Series XVII)
London: Orion Books, 1999

Der Heros in Tausend Gestalten
München: Insel Verlag, 2009

Occidental Mythology
Princeton: Princeton University Press, 1973
(Bollingen Series XVII)
New York: Penguin Arkana, 1991

The Masks of God
Oriental Mythology
New York: Penguin Arkana, 1992
Originally published 1962

Mythologie des Ostens
Die Masken Gottes Bd. 2
Basel: Sphinx Verlag, 1996

The Power of Myth
With Bill Moyers
ed. by Sue Flowers
New York: Anchor Books, 1988

Die Kraft der Mythen
Düsseldorf: Patmos Verlag, 2007

Capacchione, Lucia

The Power of Your Other Hand
North Hollywood, CA: Newcastle Publishing, 1988

Capra, Bernt Amadeus

Mindwalk
A Film for Passionate Thinkers
Based Upon Fritjof Capra's *The Turning Point*
New York: Triton Pictures, 1990

Capra, Fritjof

The Turning Point
Science, Society And The Rising Culture
New York: Simon & Schuster, 1987
Original Author Copyright, 1982

Wendezeit
Bausteine für ein neues Weltbild
München: Droemer Knaur, 2004

Le temps du changement
Science, société et nouvelle culture
Paris: Rocher, 1994

The Tao of Physics
An Exploration of the Parallels Between Modern
Physics and Eastern Mysticism
New York: Shambhala Publications, 2000
(New Edition) Originally published in 1975

Das Tao der Physik
Die Konvergenz von westlicher Wissenschaft und östlicher Philosophie
Neue und erweiterte Auflage
München: O.W. Barth bei Scherz, 2000
Ursprünglich erschienen 1975 bei Droemersche Verlagsanstalt
in Hamburg

Le tao de la physique
Paris: Sand & Tchou, 1994

The Web of Life
A New Scientific Understanding of Living Systems
New York: Doubleday, 1997
Lebensnetz
Ein neues Verständnis der lebendigen Welt
München: Scherz Verlag, 1999

The Hidden Connections
Integrating The Biological, Cognitive And Social
Dimensions Of Life Into A Science Of Sustainability
New York: Doubleday, 2002

Verborgene Zusammenhänge
München: Scherz, 2002

Steering Business Toward Sustainability
New York: United Nations University Press, 1995

Uncommon Wisdom
Conversations with Remarkable People
New York: Bantam, 1989

The Science of Leonardo
Inside the Mind of the Great Genius of the Renaissance
New York: Anchor Books, 2008
New York: Bantam Doubleday, 2007 (First Publishing)

Chopra, Deepak
Creating Affluence
The A-to-Z Steps to a Richer Life
New York: Amber-Allen Publishing (2003)

Synchrodestiny
Discover the Power of Meaningful Coincidence to Manifest Abundance
Audio Book / CD
Niles, IL: Nightingale-Conant, 2006

The Seven Spiritual Laws of Success
A Practical Guide to the Fulfillment of Your Dreams
Audio Book / CD
New York: Amber-Allen Publishing (2002)

Die Sieben Geistigen Gesetze des Erfolgs
Berlin: Ullstein Verlag, 2004

The Spontaneous Fulfillment of Desire
Harnessing the Infinite Power of Coincidence
New York: Random House Audio, 2003

Constantine, Larry L.

Children & Sex
New Findings, New Perspectives
Larry L. Constantine & Floyd M. Martinson (Eds.)
Boston: Little, Brown & Company, 1981

Treasures of the Island
Children in Alternative Lifestyles
Beverly Hills: Sage Publications, 1976

Where are the Kids?
in: Libby & Whitehurst (ed.)
Marriage and Alternatives
Glenview: Scott Foresman, 1977

Open Family
A Lifestyle for Kids and other People
26 FAMILY COORDINATOR 113-130 (1977)

Covey, Stephen R.

The 7 Habits of Highly Effective People
Powerful Lessons in Personal Change
New York: Free Press, 2004
15th Anniversary Edition
First Published in 1989

Die 7 Wege zur Effektivität
Prinzipien für persönlichen und beruflichen Erfolg
Offenbach: Gabal Verlag, 2009

The 8th Habit
From Effectiveness to Greatness
London: Simon & Schuster, 2004

Der 8. Weg
Von der Effektivität zur wahren Grösse
6. Auflage
Offenbach: Gabal Verlag, 2006

De Bono, Edward

The Use of Lateral Thinking
New York: Penguin, 1967

The Mechanism of Mind
New York: Penguin, 1969

Sur/Petition
London: HarperCollins, 1993

Tactics
London: HarperCollins, 1993
First published in 1985

Taktiken und Strategien erfolgreicher Menschen
Frankfurt/M: MVG Verlag, 1995

Serious Creativity
Using the Power of Lateral Thinking to Create New Ideas
London: HarperCollins, 1996

Dolto, Françoise

La Cause des Enfants
Paris: Laffont, 1985

Mein Leben auf der Seite der Kinder
Ein Plädoyer für eine kindgerechte Welt
Hamburg: Lübbe Verlagsgruppe, 1993

Psychanalyse et Pédiatrie
Paris: Seuil, 1971

Psychoanalyse und Kinderheilkunde
Frankfurt/M: Suhrkamp, 1997

Séminaire de Psychanalyse d'Enfants, 1
Paris: Seuil, 1982

Séminaire de Psychanalyse d'Enfants, 2
Paris: Seuil, 1985

Séminaire de Psychanalyse d'Enfants, 3
Paris: Seuil, 1988

Praxis der Kinderanalyse. Ein Seminar.
Hamburg: Klett-Cotta, 1985

Alles ist Sprache
Kindern mit Worten helfen
Berlin: Quadriga, 1996

Über das Begehren
Die Anfänge der menschlichen Kommunikation
2. Auflage
Hamburg: Klett-Cotta, 1996

Kinder stark machen
Die ersten Lebensjahre
Berlin: Beltz Verlag, 2000

L'évangile au risque de la psychanalyse
Paris: Seuil, 1980

Dürckheim, Karlfried Graf

Hara: The Vital Center of Man
Rochester: Inner Traditions, 2004

Hara
Die Erdmitte des Menschen
Neuausgabe
München: O.W. Barth bei Scherz, 2005

Zen and Us
New York: Penguin Arkana 1991

The Call for the Master
New York: Penguin Books, 1993

Absolute Living
The Otherworldly in the World and the Path to Maturity
New York: Penguin Arkana, 1992

The Way of Transformation
Daily Life as a Spiritual Exercise
London: Allen & Unwin, 1988

Der Alltag als Übung
Vom Weg der Verwandlung
Bern: Huber, 2008

The Japanese Cult of Tranquility
London: Rider, 1960

Kultur der Stille
Frankfurt/M: Weltz Verlag, 1997

Goleman, Daniel

Emotional Intelligence
New York, Bantam Books, 1995

EQ. Emotionale Intelligenz
München: DTV Verlag, 1997

Goswami, Amit

The Self-Aware Universe
How Consciousness Creates the Material World
New York: Tarcher/Putnam, 1995

Das Bewusste Universum
Wie Bewusstsein die materielle Welt erschafft
Stuttgart: Lüchow Verlag, 2007

Greene, Liz

Astrology of Fate
York Beach, ME: Red Wheel/Weiser, 1986

Saturn
A New Look at an Old Devil
York Beach, ME: Red Wheel/Weiser, 1976

The Astrological Neptune and the Quest for Redemption
Boston: Red Wheel Weiser, 1996

The Mythic Journey
With Juliet Sharman-Burke
The Meaning of Myth as a Guide for Life
New York: Simon & Schuster (Fireside), 2000

Die Mythische Reise
Die Bedeutung der Mythen als ein Führer durch das Leben
München: Atmosphären Verlag, 2004

The Mythic Tarot
With Juliet Sharman-Burke
New York: Simon & Schuster (Fireside), 2001
Originally published in 1986

Le Tarot Mythique
Une nouvelle approche du Tarot
Paris: Solar, 1988

The Luminaries
The Psychology of the Sun and Moon in the Horoscope
With Howard Sasportas
York Beach, ME: Red Wheel/Weiser, 1992

Sonne und Mond
Die Bedeutung der grossen Lichter in der Mythologie und im Horoskop
Saarbrücken: Neue Erde/Lentz, 2000

Greer, John Michael

Earth Divination, Earth Magic
A Practical Guide to Geomancy
New York: Llewellyn Publications, 1999

Hicks, Esther and Jerry

The Amazing Power of Deliberate Intent
Living the Art of Allowing
Carlsbad, CA: Hay House, 2006

Holmes, Ernst

The Science of Mind
A Philosophy, A Faith, A Way of Life
New York: Jeremy P. Tarcher/Putnam, 1998
First Published in 1938

Houston, Jean

The Possible Human
A Course in Enhancing Your Physical, Mental, and Creative Abilities
New York: Jeremy P. Tarcher/Putnam, 1982

Huang, Alfred

The Complete I Ching
The Definite Translation from Taoist Master Alfred Huang
Rochester, NY: Inner Traditions, 1998

Hunt, Valerie

Infinite Mind
Science of the Human Vibrations of Consciousness
Malibu, CA: Malibu Publishing, 2000

Huxley, Aldous

The Doors of Perception and Heaven and Hell
London: HarperCollins (Flamingo), 1994
(originally published in 1954)

The Perennial Philosophy
San Francisco: Harper & Row, 1970

Jackson, Stevi

Childhood and Sexuality
New York: Blackwell, 1982

Jung, Carl Gustav

Archetypen
München: DTV Verlag, 2001

Archetypes of the Collective Unconscious
in: The Basic Writings of C.G. Jung
New York: The Modern Library, 1959, 358-407

Collected Works
New York, 1959

Dialectique du moi et de l'inconscient
Paris, Gallimard, 1991

On the Nature of the Psyche
in: The Basic Writings of C.G. Jung
New York: The Modern Library, 1959, 47-133

Psychological Types
Collected Writings, Vol. 6
Princeton: Princeton University Press, 1971

Psychologie und Religion
München: DTV Verlag, 2001

Psychology and Religion
in: The Basic Writings of C.G. Jung
New York: The Modern Library, 1959, 582-655

Religious and Psychological Problems of Alchemy
in: The Basic Writings of C.G. Jung
New York: The Modern Library, 1959, 537-581

Symbol und Libido
Freiburg: Walter Verlag, 1987

Synchronizität, Akausalität und Okkultismus
Frankfurt/M: DTV, 2001

The Basic Writings of C.G. Jung
New York: The Modern Library, 1959

The Development of Personality
Collected Writings, Vol. 17
Princeton: Princeton University Press, 1954

The Meaning and Significance of Dreams
Boston: Sigo Press, 1991

The Myth of the Divine Child
in: Essays on A Science of Mythology
Princeton, N.J.: Princeton University Press Bollingen
Series XXII, 1969. (With Karl Kerenyi)

Traum und Traumdeutung
München: DTV Verlag, 2001

Two Essays on Analytical Psychology
Collected Writings, Vol. 7
Princeton: Princeton University Press, 1972
First published by Routledge & Kegan Paul, Ltd., 1953

Zur Psychologie westlicher und östlicher Religion
Fünfte Auflage
Olten: Walter Verlag, 1988

Kiang, Kok Kok

The I Ching
An Illustrated Guide to the Chinese Art of Divination
Singapore: Asiapac, 1993

Krishnamurti, J.

Freedom From The Known
San Francisco: Harper & Row, 1969

The First and Last Freedom
San Francisco: Harper & Row, 1975

Education and the Significance of Life
London: Victor Gollancz, 1978

Commentaries on Living
First Series
London: Victor Gollancz, 1985
Commentaries on Living
Second Series
London: Victor Gollancz, 1986

Krishnamurti's Journal
London: Victor Gollancz, 1987

Krishnamurti's Notebook
London: Victor Gollancz, 1986

Beyond Violence
London: Victor Gollancz, 1985

Beginnings of Learning
New York: Penguin, 1986

The Penguin Krishnamurti Reader
New York: Penguin, 1987

On God
San Francisco: Harper & Row, 1992

On Fear
San Francisco: Harper & Row, 1995

The Essential Krishnamurti
San Francisco: Harper & Row, 1996

The Ending of Time
With Dr. David Bohm
San Francisco: Harper & Row, 1985

Leonard, George, Murphy, Michael

The Live We Are Given
A Long Term Program for Realizing the
Potential of Body, Mind, Heart and Soul
New York: Jeremy P. Tarcher/Putnam, 1984

Liedloff, Jean

Continuum Concept
In Search of Happiness Lost
New York: Perseus Books, 1986
First published in 1977

Auf der Suche nach dem verlorenen Glück
Gegen die Zerstörung der Glücksfähigkeit in der frühen Kindheit
München: C.H. Beck Verlag, 2006

Lowen, Alexander

Angst vor dem Leben
Über den Ursprung seelischen Leides und den Weg
zu einem reicheren Dasein
München: Goldmann Wilhelm, 1989

Bioenergetics
New York: Coward, McGoegham 1975

Bioenergetik
Therapie der Seele durch Arbeit mit dem Körper
Berlin: Rowohlt, 2008

Depression and the Body
The Biological Basis of Faith and Reality
New York: Penguin, 1992

Fear of Life
New York: Bioenergetic Press, 2003

Honoring the Body
The Autobiography of Alexander Lowen
New York: Bioenergetic Press, 2004

Joy
The Surrender to the Body and to Life
New York: Penguin, 1995

Love and Orgasm
New York: Macmillan, 1965

Love, Sex and Your Heart
New York: Bioenergetics Press, 2004

Narcissism: Denial of the True Self
New York: Macmillan, Collier Books, 1983

Narzissmus
Die Verleugnung des wahren Selbst
München: Goldmann Wilhelm, 1992

Pleasure: A Creative Approach to Life
New York: Bioenergetics Press, 2004
First published in 1970

The Language of the Body
Physical Dynamics of Character Structure
New York: Bioenergetics Press, 2006

Maharshi, Ramana

The Collected Works of Ramana Maharshi
New York: Sri Ramanasramam, 2002

The Essential Teachings of Ramana Maharshi
A Visual Journey
New York: Inner Directions Publishing, 2002
by Matthew Greenblad

Sei was du bist!
München: O.W. Barth, 2001

Nan Yar? Wer bin ich?
München: Kamphausen, 2002

Malinowski, Bronislaw

Crime und Custom in Savage Society
London: Kegan, 1926

Sex and Repression in Savage Society
London: Kegan, 1927

The Sexual Life of Savages in North West Melanesia
New York: Halycon House, 1929

Das Geschlechtsleben der Wilden in Nordwest-Melanesien
Liebe, Ehe und Familienleben bei den Eingeborenen der
Trobriand Inseln, Britisch-Neuguinea
Eschborn: Klotz Verlag, 2005

Martinson, Floyd M.

Sexual Knowledge
Values and Behavior Patterns
St. Peter: Minn.: Gustavus Adolphus College, 1966

Infant and Child Sexuality
St. Peter: Minn.: Gustavus Adolphus College, 1973

The Quality of Adolescent Experiences
St. Peter: Minn.: Gustavus Adolphus College, 1974

The Child and the Family
Calgary, Alberta: The University of Calgary, 1980

The Sex Education of Young Children
in: Lorna Brown (Ed.), *Sex Education in the Eighties*
New York, London: Plenum Press, 1981, pp. 51 ff.

The Sexual Life of Children
New York: Bergin & Garvey, 1994

Children and Sex, Part II: Childhood Sexuality
in: Bullough & Bullough, Human Sexuality (1994)
Pp. 111-116

McKenna, Terence

The Archaic Revival
San Francisco: Harper & Row, 1992

Food of The Gods
A Radical History of Plants, Drugs and Human Evolution
London: Rider, 1992

Die Speisen der Götter
Berlin: Synergia/Syntropia, 1996

The Invisible Landscape
Mind Hallucinogens and the I Ching
New York: HarperCollins, 1993
(With Dennis McKenna)

True Hallucinations
Being the Account of the Author's Extraordinary
Adventures in the Devil's Paradise
New York: Fine Communications, 1998

McNiff, Shaun

Art as Medicine
Boston: Shambhala, 1992

Art as Therapy
Creating a Therapy of the Imagination
Boston/London: Shambhala, 1992

Trust the Process
An Artist's Guide to Letting Go
New York: Shambhala Publications, 1998

Miller, Mary & Taube, Karl

An Illustrated Dictionary of the Gods and Symbols of Ancient Mexico and the Maya
London: Thames & Hudson, 1993

Montessori, Maria

The Absorbent Mind
Reprint Edition
New York: Buccaneer Books, 1995
First published in 1973

Das Kreative Kind
Der absorbierende Geist
Freiburg: Herder, 2007

Moore, Thomas

Care of the Soul
A Guide for Cultivating Depth and Sacredness in Everyday Life
New York: Harper & Collins, 1994

Die Seele Lieben
Tiefe und Spiritualität im täglichen Leben
München: Droemer Knaur, 1995

Murphy, Joseph

The Power of Your Subconscious Mind
West Nyack, N.Y.: Parker, 1981, N.Y.: Bantam, 1982
Originally published in 1962

Die Macht Ihres Unterbewusstseins
München: Hugendubel, 2000

La puissance de votre subconscient
Genève: Ramón Keller, 1967

The Miracle of Mind Dynamics
New York: Prentice Hall, 1964

Miracle Power for Infinite Riches
West Nyack, N.Y.: Parker, 1972

The Amazing Laws of Cosmic Mind Power
West Nyack, N.Y.: Parker, 1973

Secrets of the I Ching
West Nyack, N.Y.: Parker, 1970

Think Yourself Rich
Use the Power of Your Subconscious Mind to Find True Wealth
Revised by Ian D. McMahan, Ph.D.
Paramus, NJ: Reward Books, 2001

Das Erfolgsbuch
Wie sie alles im Leben erreichen können
Hamburg: Heyne Verlag, 2002

Wahrheiten die ihr Leben verändern
Dr. Joseph Murphys Vermächtnis
München: Hugendubel, 1996

Murphy, Michael

The Future of the Body
Explorations into the Further Evolution of Human Nature
New York: Jeremy P. Tarcher/Putnam, 1992

Der Quanten-Mensch
München: Ludwig Verlag, 1996

Myers, Tony Pearce

The Soul of Creativity
Insights into the Creative Process
Novato, CA: New World Library, 1999

Narby, Jeremy

The Cosmic Serpent
DNA and the Origins of Knowledge
New York: J. P. Tarcher, 1999

Die Kosmische Schlange
Auf den Pfaden der Schamanen zu den Ursprüngen modernen Wissens
Stuttgart: Klett-Cotta, 2007

Nau, Erika

Self-Awareness Through Huna
Virginia Beach: Donning, 1981

Selbstbewusst durch Huna
Die magische Weisheit Hawaiis
2. Auflage
Basel: Sphinx Verlag, 1989

Neill, Alexander Sutherland

Neill! Neill! Orange-Peel!
New York: Hart Publishing Co., 1972

Neill! Neill! Birnenstiel!
Berlin: Rowohlt, 1973

Summerhill
A Radical Approach to Child Rearing
New York: Hart Publishing, Reprint 1984
Originally published 1960

Theorie und Praxis der Antiautoritären Erziehung
Das Beispiel Summerhill
Berlin: Rowohlt Verlag, 1969

Summerhill School
A New View of Childhood
New York: St. Martin's Press
Reprint 1995

Das Prinzip Summerhill
Berlin: Rowohlt, 1971

Ni, Hua-Ching

I Ching
The Book of Changes and the Unchanging Truth
2nd edition
Santa Barbara: Seven Star Communications, 1999

Esoteric Tao The Ching
The Shrine of the Eternal Breath of Tao
Santa Monica: College of Tao and Traditional
Chinese Healing, 1992

The Complete Works of Lao Tzu
Tao The Ching & Hua Hu Ching
Translation and Elucidation by Hua-Ching Ni
Santa Monica: Seven Star Communications, 1995

Nichols, Sallie

Jung and Tarot: An Archetypal Journey
New York: Red Wheel/Weiser, 1986

Die Psychologie des Tarot
Interlaken: Ansata Verlag, 1996

Ostrander, Sheila & Schroeder, Lynn

Superlearning 2000
New York: Delacorte Press, 1994

Superlearning
Die revolutionäre Lernmethode
München: Scherz Verlag, 1979

Supermemory
New York: Carroll & Graf, 1991

SuperMemory
Der Weg zum optimalen Gedächtnis
München: Goldmann, 1996

Radin, Dean

The Conscious Universe
The Scientific Truth of Psychic Phenomena
San Francisco: Harper & Row, 1997

Entangled Minds
Extrasensory Experiences in a Quantum Reality
New York: Paraview Pocket Books, 2006

Roberts, Jane

The Nature of Personal Reality
New York: Amber-Allen Publishing, 1994
First published in 1974

Die Natur der Persönlichen Realität
Ein neues Bewusstsein als Quelle der Kreativität
München: Kailash Verlag, 2007

The Nature of the Psyche
Its Human Expression
New York, Amber-Allen Publishing, 1996
First published in 1979

Die Natur der Psyche
Ihr menschlicher Ausdruck in Kreativität, Liebe, Sexualität
Genf: Ariston Verlag, 1985

Die Natur der Psyche
Ihr menschlicher Ausdruck in Kreativität, Liebe, Sexualität
München: Kailash Verlag, 2008

Rudhyar, Dane

Astrology of Personality
A Reformulation of Astrological Concepts and Ideals in
Terms of Contemporary Psychology and Philosophy
New York: Aurora Press, 1990

An Astrological Triptych
Gifts of the Spirit, The Way Through, and The Illumined Road
New York: Aurora Press, 1991

Astrological Mandala
New York: Vintage Books, 1994

L'astrologie de la transformation
Paris: Rocher, 1984

Ruiz, Don Miguel

The Four Agreements
A Practical Guide to Personal Freedom
San Rafael, CA: Amber Allen Publishing, 1997

The Mastery of Love
A Practical Guide to the Art of Relationship
San Rafael, CA: Amber Allen Publishing, 1999

The Voice of Knowledge
A Practical Guide to Inner Peace
San Rafael, CA: Amber Allen Publishing, 2004

Ruperti, Alexander

Cycles of Becoming
The Planetary Pattern of Growth
New York: CRCS Publications, 1978

Sheldrake, Rupert

A New Science of Life
The Hypothesis of Morphic Resonance
Rochester: Park Street Press, 1995

Das Schöpferische Universum
Die Theorie des morphogenetischen Feldes
Neue und erweiterte Auflage
Berlin: Ullstein, 2009

Shone, Ronald

Creative Visualization
Using Imagery and Imagination for Self-Transformation
New York: Destiny Books, 1998

Smith, C. Michael

Jung and Shamanism in Dialogue
London: Trafford Publishing, 2007

Spiller, Jan

Astrology for the Soul
New York: Bantam, 1997

Steiner, Rudolf

Theosophy
An Introduction to the Spiritual Processes in Human Life
and in the Cosmos
New York: Anthroposophic Press, 1994

Die Erziehung des Kindes
Dornach: Rudolf Steiner Verlag, 2003
First published in 1907

Thorsson, Edred

Futhark
A Handbook of Rune Magic
San Francisco: Weiser Books, 1984

Tolle, Eckhart

The Power of Now
A Guide to Spiritual Enlightenment
Novato, CA: New World Library, 2004

Jetzt! Die Kraft der Gegenwart
Ein Leitfaden zum spirituellen Erwachen
Bielefeld: Kamphausen Verlag, 2000

A New Earth
Awakening to Your Life's Purpose
New York: Michael Joseph (Penguin), 2005

Eine neue Erde
Bewusstseinssprung anstelle von Selbstzerstörung
München: Goldmann, 2005

Wild, Leon D.

The Runes Workbook
A Step-by-Step Guide to Learning the Wisdom of the Staves
San Diego: Thunder Bay Press, 2004

Wilhelm Helmut

The Wilhelm Lectures on the Book of Changes
Princeton: Princeton University Press, 1995

Wilhelm, Richard

The I Ching or Book of Changes
With C. Baynes
3rd Edition, Bollingen Series XIX
Princeton, NJ: Princeton University Press, 1967

Williams, Strephon Kaplan

Dreams and Spiritual Growth
With Patricia H. Berne and Louis M. Savary
New York: Paulist Press, 1984

Durch Traumarbeit zum eigenen Selbst
Die Jung-Senoi Methode
Interlaken: Ansata Verlag, 1987

Dream Cards
Understand Your Dreams and Enrich Your Life
New York: Simon & Schuster (Fireside), 1991

Wing, R. L.

The I Ching Workbook
Garden City, N.Y.: Doubleday, 1984

Das Arbeitsbuch zum I Ching
Mit Chinesischen Orakel Münzen
München: Goldmann, 2004

Het I Tjing Werkboek
Baarn: Bigot & Van Rossum, 1986

Wolf, Fred Alan

Taking the Quantum Leap
The New Physics for Nonscientists
New York: Harper & Row, 1989

Der Quantensprung ist keine Hexerei
Frankfurt/M: Fischer Verlag, 1990

Parallel Universes
New York: Simon & Schuster, 1990

The Dreaming Universe
A Mind-Expanding Journey into the Realm
Where Psyche and Physics Meet
New York: Touchstone, 1995

The Eagle's Quest
A Physicist Finds the Scientific Truth At the Heart of the Shamanic World
New York: Touchstone, 1997

Die Physik der Träume
Frankfurt/M: DTV Verlag, 1997

Mind into Matter
A New Alchemy of Science and Spirit
New York: Moment Point Press, 2000

Voice Dialogue is not a school of psychotherapy, it is not a substitute for psychotherapy, and it is not a profession in and of itself. It is a technique for psychological exploration and for the expansion of awareness. Although it can be a highly effective tool for any psychotherapist it should be clearly understood that it is not a complete and autonomous therapeutic system.

– Hal & Sidra Stone, Embracing Ourselves (1989), p. 78

FROM THE SAME AUTHOR

A Bibliography

You can search publications from here:
http://ipublica.com/books/

For audio books and music, you can start here:
http://ipublica.com/audio/

All paperbacks, audio downloads, audio book compact discs, music downloads and music compact discs, as well as Kindle books, are referenced on the site.

For free podcasts search iTunes under my author name.

For quoting my publications, please use the following form:
Pierre F. Walter, [Title]: [Subtitle], Newark: Sirius-C Media Galaxy LLC, 2011

Web Presence

Pierre F. Walter on the Web

Sites

http://authoryourlife.com

http://ipublica.com

http://ipublica.net

http://ipublica.org

http://ipublica.tv

Video Channels

http://youtube.com/user/ipublica

http://youtube.com/user/authoryourlife

http://vimeo.com/pierrefwalter/channels

http://ipublica.blip.tv/

http://authoryourlife.blip.tv/

http://emosexuality.blip.tv/

http://pierrefwalter.blip.tv/